# ATLAS OF WORLD FAITHS

# CHRISTIANITY

## Jane Bingham

**Smart Apple Media**

This book has been published in cooperation with Arcturus Publishing Limited.

Series concept: Alex Woolf
Editor and picture researcher: Alex Woolf
Designer: Simon Borrough
Cartography: Encompass Graphics
Consultant: Douglas G. Heming

Picture credits:
Art Archive: 17 (Jan Vinchon Numismatist, Paris/Dagli Orti), 23 (Abbey of Monteoliveto Maggiore Siena/Dagli Orti [A]), 25 (British Library), 33.
Corbis: cover (Oswaldo Rivas/Reuters), 5 (Gianni Dagli Orti), 6 (Brooklyn Museum), 9 (National Gallery, London), 10 (Archivo Iconográfico, S.A.), 12–13 (Eric and David Hosking), 15 (Archivo Iconográfico, S.A.), 18 (Archivo Iconográfico, S.A.), 21 (David Samuel Robbins), 27 (Archivo Iconográfico, S.A.), 28 (James L. Amos), 31 (Eric Crichton), 35 (Bettmann), 36 (Underwood & Underwood), 39 (Bettmann), 40 (You Sung-Ho/Reuters).

Published in the United States by Smart Apple Media
2140 Howard Drive West, North Mankato, Minnesota 56003

Library of Congress Cataloging-in-Publication Data

Bingham, Jane.
Christianity / by Jane Bingham.
p. cm.—(Atlas of world faiths)
Includes index.
ISBN 978-1-59920-054-5
1. Christianity. 2. Church history. I. Title. II. Series.

BR121.3.B56 2007
270—dc22          2007007533

9 8 7 6 5 4 3 2 1

# CONTENTS

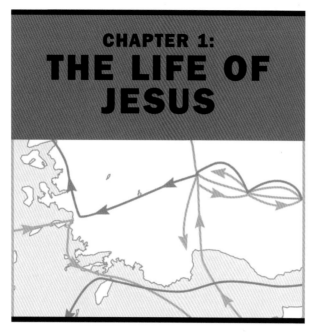

# CHAPTER 1: THE LIFE OF JESUS

The Christian religion began with the life of Jesus of Nazareth in the first century CE. Christians believe that Jesus is the Son of God. They teach that God sent Jesus to the earth to save people from their sins and to teach them how to live good lives by following God's commandments. Jesus lived in Palestine, in the Middle East. Christians often call the region where Jesus lived the "Holy Land." Most of this area is now part of Israel.

Jesus was born around the year 4 in the kingdom of Judaea. This was the ancestral home of the Jewish people, but by the time of Jesus's birth, it was part of the Roman Empire. The emperor Augustus ruled the empire when Jesus was born, but Augustus allowed a local King, named Herod, to govern Judaea according to Roman laws. Herod ruled from 37 BCE to 4 CE.

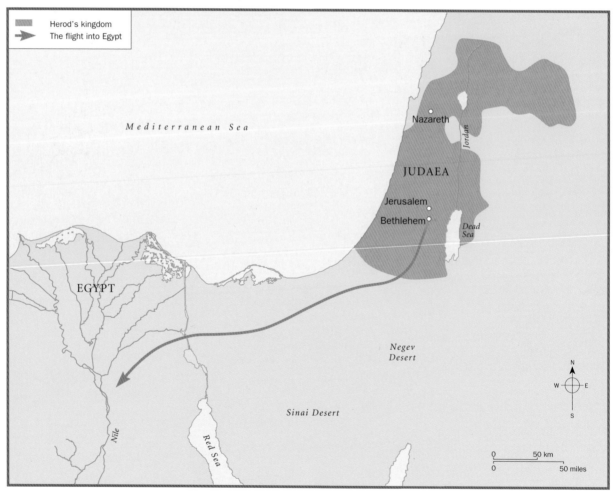

**King Herod's kingdom at the time of the birth of Jesus. This map also shows the route that Jesus's family followed when they escaped from Judaea into Egypt.**

Bethlehem, 99 miles (160 km) to the south. They had to make this journey because Emperor Augustus had decreed that everyone in the Roman Empire must return to their birthplace to be registered. The Bible tells how Jesus was born in a Bethlehem stable because all the inns in the town were full.

## The flight into Egypt

After Jesus was born, kings from the east arrived to see the baby Jesus. According to the Bible, the kings—also called "wise men"—traveled from countries east of Palestine, guided by a bright star. Before they reached Bethlehem, the wise men visited King Herod in Jerusalem to ask about the newborn, calling the baby a "king." The news of Jesus's birth made Herod jealous and he ordered the murder of all the baby boys in his kingdom, hoping that Jesus would be killed.

Herod's plan to kill the baby Jesus did not succeed. Joseph was warned by an angel in a dream, and he and his family fled Bethlehem and traveled to Egypt. This long and difficult journey involved crossing the Negev and Sinai deserts. Christians refer to this journey as the "Flight into Egypt."

According to the Bible, the first people to visit the baby Jesus were local shepherds, who were told about Jesus's birth by an angel. The shepherds brought lambs as gifts for the baby. This painting, called the *Adoration of the Shepherds*, is by the seventeenth-century Spanish artist, Bartolomé Murillo.

## The birth of Jesus

The birth of Jesus is described in the Bible. The story begins with the Annunciation, when the Angel Gabriel appeared to a woman named Mary—known to Christians as the Virgin Mary—telling her she would give birth to the Son of God. The Annunciation took place at Mary's home in the village of Nazareth, in a hilly northern region of Palestine called Galilee.

Just before Jesus was born, Mary and her husband Joseph set off on a journey to Joseph's hometown of

## THE BIBLE

The Bible is divided into two main sections. The Old Testament tells the history of the Jewish people; the New Testament describes the life of Jesus and how his followers spread the Christian religion. The New Testament includes four books, called the Gospels, which tell the story of the life of Jesus. Each Gospel tells a slightly different version of Jesus's life, because the Gospels are believed to have been written by four different men—Matthew, Mark, Luke, and John.

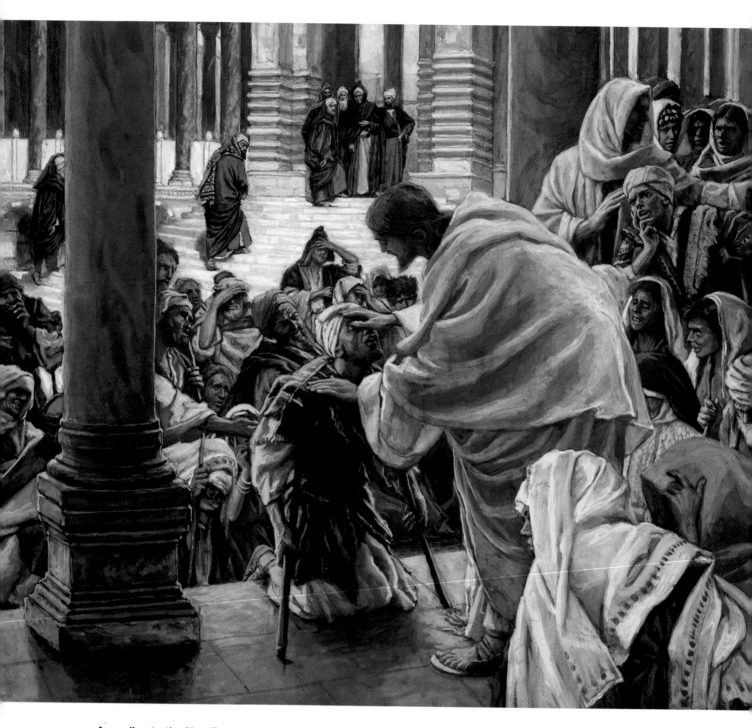

According to the New Testament, wherever Jesus traveled, he performed miracles and attracted many followers. Here, Jesus is shown outside the Temple in Jerusalem curing a man of his disability, while the temple priests suspiciously look on.

## The life and works of Jesus

Jesus and his family stayed in Egypt until Herod died and it was safe to return to Nazareth. Jesus spent his childhood in Nazareth, where Joseph taught him carpentry. Sometimes his family visited Jerusalem for important Jewish festivals.

Most of the events in Jesus's adult life occurred around the Sea of Galilee, a large freshwater lake on the Jordan River. In this mountainous area, Jesus traveled from place to place, teaching, healing the sick, and performing miracles. He attracted followers, known as disciples.

On the banks of the Sea of Galilee, Jesus called his disciples to leave their fishing nets and follow him. Matthew's Gospel says that Jesus stopped a storm on the sea, and then he walked on the water.

One of Jesus's most famous miracles took place at Bethsaida, on the shores of Galilee. Here, Jesus turned five loaves and two fish into enough food to feed a crowd of 5,000 people. Across the sea, in Capernaum, Jesus performed several healing miracles. Traveling west to the town of Cana, he turned water into wine at a wedding feast.

The Bible says that Jesus preached wherever he went; his most famous teaching is called the Sermon on the Mount. Most archaeologists believe that Jesus gave this sermon on a hill close to Capernaum, overlooking the Sea of Galilee. Today, this hill is known as the Mount of the Beatitudes.

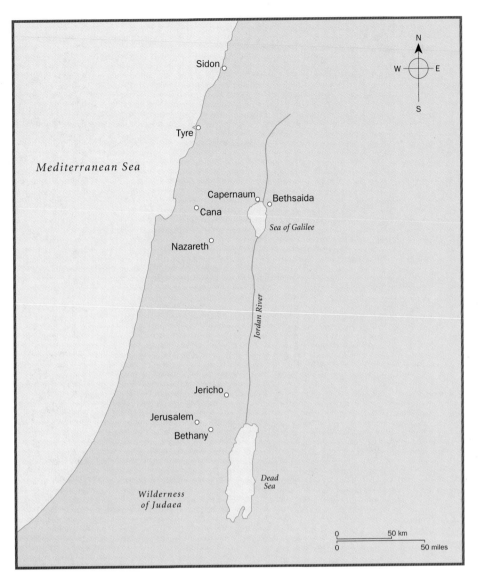

A map of Palestine, showing some of the places where Jesus preached. Jesus spent most of his time around the Sea of Galilee, but he also traveled as far north as Sidon and as far south as Bethany.

## JESUS IN THE WILDERNESS

According to Matthew's Gospel, before Jesus began his work as a preacher, he spent 40 days and 40 nights in the harsh, rocky wilderness of Judaea, south of Jerusalem. There he struggled with many temptations. Matthew describes how the Devil tempted Jesus to give up his holy way of life in exchange for a life of comfort, power, and riches. Jesus resisted these temptations. Every year, Christians remember Jesus's time in the wilderness during the season of Lent that lasts for 40 days until just before Easter.

**Jesus's travels** The Bible describes several journeys that Jesus took with his disciples. He traveled as far north as the ports of Tyre and Sidon and as far south as Jerusalem and Bethany. Jesus also spent some time in Bethany, a village close to Jerusalem. This was the home of his friends Mary, Martha, and their brother Lazarus. The Gospel of John tells how Lazarus died and then was miraculously brought back to life by Jesus.

Mount of
Olives

City gate

Garden of
Gethsemane

Hill of
Calvary

The
Temple

City wall

Herod's
Palace

Probable site of the upper room
where the Last Supper was held

## THE LAST SUPPER

Not long before he was arrested, Jesus shared a
special meal with all of his disciples. This meal,
known as the Last Supper, was held in an upper
room of a house in Jerusalem. At the Last Supper,
Jesus instructed his followers to share bread and
wine in memory of him. He explained that the
bread and wine were his body and blood. This
was the start of the service of Holy Communion,
which is practiced by all Christians. Holy
Communion is also known as the Eucharist or
the Mass.

**A plan of Jerusalem, showing some of the places
associated with the last few weeks of Jesus's life.**

In the last weeks of his life, Jesus traveled to Jerusalem.
When he reached a hill called the Mount of Olives near
Jerusalem, Jesus sent two disciples to find a donkey so
that he could ride into the city. The people of Jerusalem
welcomed Jesus. They sang songs and cut down
branches from palm trees to lay in his path.

**Preaching and arrest** For the next few
weeks, Jesus preached in Jerusalem and cured the sick.
People flocked to see him, praising him as the Son of
God. This made the local religious authorities—called

priests—very unhappy, especially when Jesus taught in their Temple.

Eventually, the priests decided to take action. They persuaded one of the disciples, Judas Iscariot, to betray Jesus. One evening, Judas led a group of soldiers to the Garden of Gethsemane, on the slopes of the Mount of Olives. Jesus was walking in the garden when Judas approached him and gave him a kiss. This was a sign for the soldiers to arrest Jesus.

## Crucifixion and Resurrection

Jesus was put on trial by the priests and then taken to be sentenced by Pontius Pilate, the Roman governor of Judaea. The priests wanted Pilate to order Jesus's execution. However, Pilate could not find a reason to put Jesus to death, so he asked the crowd that had gathered to witness the sentencing to choose who should be crucified, Jesus or a thief named Barabas.

By this time, the crowd had turned against Jesus, and they decided that he should be crucified. Jesus was given a crown of thorns and forced to carry a heavy wooden cross to a hill called Calvary, just outside the city walls. There, he was crucified between two thieves. Calvary is also known as Golgotha, which means "the place of the skull."

The body of Jesus was placed in a tomb cut out of a rock face, and the tomb was sealed with a heavy stone. However, three days later one of Jesus's followers, Mary Magdalene, discovered that the stone had been rolled to one side and the tomb was empty. She was afraid that Jesus's body had been stolen, but the Bible says that Jesus appeared to Mary Magdalene and told her he would soon be with God, his Father, in heaven. This "rising from the dead" is called the Resurrection.

**The Crucifixion has been painted by famous artists. This painting is by the Italian artist Raphael (1483–1520). It is called *The Crucified Christ with the Virgin Mary, Saints, and Angels*.**

# CHAPTER 2: SPREADING THE WORD

**A**fter Jesus's death, his disciples continued to spread his message. They referred to him as Jesus Christ. "Christ" comes from the Greek word *Christos*, meaning the "Annointed One." The disciples taught that Christ had died to save people from their sins and to give them the chance to go to heaven. They told people to follow Christ and to live a virtuous life, obeying Christ's teachings. The followers of Christ who spread Christianity are known as the apostles. Their work is described in a section of the New Testament called the Acts of the Apostles.

**Pentecost** The Acts of the Apostles describes how the Holy Spirit appeared to the apostles and gave them inspiration to carry out their work. About two months after the death of Jesus, the apostles met in Jerusalem to celebrate the Jewish

## THE TRINITY

Christians believe that God has three forms: God the Father; God the Son; and God the Holy Spirit. Together, these forms of God are known as the Trinity. God the Son is Jesus Christ. God the Holy Spirit is also known as the Holy Ghost. In Christian art, the Holy Spirit is depicted as a flame or a white dove.

The martyrdom of Saint Stephen, as seen through the eyes of a sixteenth-century Spanish artist. Stephen is surrounded by tormenters who are eagerly leading him to his death.

**This map shows the main Christian centers at the end of the first century. It also shows the areas where Jewish people lived. At this time, most converts to Christianity were Jewish.**

harvest festival known as Pentecost. Suddenly, they heard the sound of a powerful wind. Then they saw a flame flickering over each of their heads, which they believed was a sign that the Holy Spirit was with them.

The apostles discovered they were able to speak in many different languages. They ventured into crowds of people and began to preach. At that time, Jerusalem was full of Jewish people who had come from many different lands to celebrate Pentecost. The apostles spoke to them all in their own languages and told them about Jesus's message.

## The message spreads

The apostles began to travel and spread the word. Gradually, the message of Christianity reached all the areas of the world where Judaism was followed. Small communities of Christians were established throughout the Middle East. At first, only Jews converted to Christianity, but slowly, Christianity also spread to Gentiles (non-Jews).

## Dying for their faith

The apostles made many enemies as they spread their new religion. In particular, Jewish leaders, known as the elders, were very angry that their people were abandoning Judaism. Some of the apostles were put to death for preaching Christianity and disobeying the commands of the elders. Stephen was stoned to death outside the walls of Jerusalem. Peter was thrown into prison and later sentenced to death.

People who die for their faith are called martyrs. Stephen and Peter were among the first of many Christian martyrs. After their deaths, they became known as Saint Stephen and Saint Peter. Saint (oftened shortened to St.) is the title given to holy people in the Christian religion.

## The conversion of Saul
One of the most important figures in the early history of Christianity is St. Paul. Paul did not start his life as a Christian. As a young man he was named Saul, and he took part in the Jewish persecution of the Christians. He even joined in the stoning of Stephen.

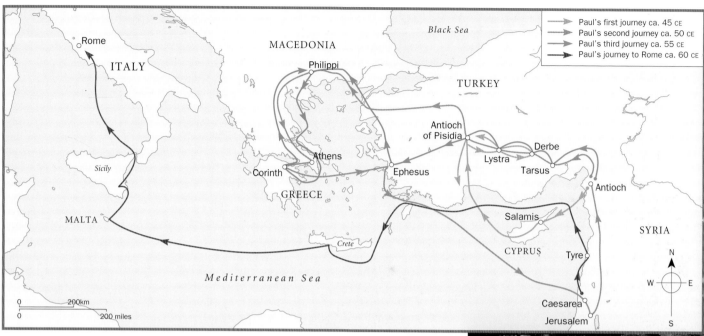

**The journeys of Saint Paul. For 25 years, Paul undertook tiring and dangerous journeys over land and sea.**

The Acts of the Apostles describes how Saul was converted to Christianity on the road from Jerusalem to Damascus in northern Palestine. As he approached Damascus, Saul had a vision of brilliant light that left him blind for three days. After he had recovered his sight, Saul became a Christian and changed his name to Paul. He spent the rest of his life traveling and spreading the Christian message.

## Paul's first journey

On Paul's first journey, he roamed the lands near the eastern Mediterranean Sea. He went to the island of Cyprus and established a church in the city of Salamis. Then, Paul returned to the mainland and traveled the areas that are now Syria and Turkey. In some places, such as Lystra, Paul was welcomed. In others, he was driven away.

## Paul's second and third journeys

On his second journey, Paul traveled to the cities of Tarsus, Lystra, and Antioch (in present-day Turkey). Then he crossed the sea to Philippi (in Macedonia), Athens, Corinth (in Greece), and Ephesus (in Turkey). In all these places, Paul established new communities of Christians.

On his third journey, Paul returned to some of the places he had visited before. While he was in Ephesus, he tried to discourage people from worshipping the goddess Artemis, also known as Diana. This made many people very angry.

## Paul's last journey

Paul was arrested when he returned to Jerusalem. The Roman rulers in Jerusalem sent him to Rome to be tried by the emperor. Paul traveled under guard in a merchant ship that was wrecked off the coast of the island of Malta.

When he finally reached Rome, Paul was placed under house arrest. During his confinement, Paul continued to preach the Christian message by writing many letters. It is uncertain how Paul died; one theory suggests he may have been beheaded by order of Emperor Nero.

## PAUL'S LETTERS

While he was traveling, Paul wrote letters to the Christian communities he had established. These letters encouraged the new Christians in their faith and taught them more about their religion. Later, Paul's letters were included in the New Testament.

Perhaps the most famous of all Paul's letters are his Letters to the Corinthians, which include a well-known passage about love. In this passage, Paul explains that Christians should love all people, Christian and non-Christian: "Above all, remember that without love, you are nothing."

The ancient theater at Ephesus in Turkey was the scene of a protest against Saint Paul. Some worshippers of the goddess Diana organized the protest against Paul's teachings, but fortunately, the crowd was kept under control.

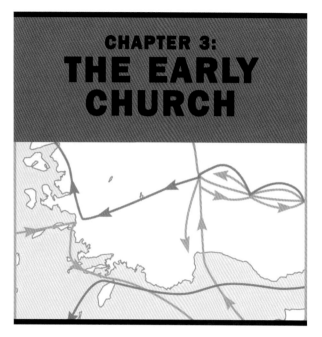

# CHAPTER 3:
# THE EARLY CHURCH

**B**y the end of the first century, Christianity was flourishing in many parts of the Roman Empire. The new faith was especially popular in Rome, but many powerful Romans were suspicious of Christianity, so most early Christians did not reveal their faith.

The early Christians met secretly in people's homes. They usually met on a Sunday, early in the morning or in the evening. The Christians prayed together, sang hymns (songs praising God), and studied the scriptures (the books of the New Testament). They also celebrated Holy Communion, as a reminder of Christ's Last Supper and his death and resurrection.

**Terrible punishments** Some Roman emperors saw Christianity as a serious threat to their power. They took harsh measures to wipe out the new religion. In 64 CE, Emperor Nero blamed the Christians for the Great Fire of Rome. Some Christians were wrapped in animal skins and thrown to the dogs, while others were used as human torches at the emperor's parties. Nero also turned killing Christians into public entertainment; Christians were sent into the arenas of public amphitheaters to be attacked and eaten by starving lions.

Other Roman emperors also had Christians arrested, tortured, and killed, but Emperor Diocletian carried out the most savage persecution. In the year 303,

**By the end of the third century, there were Christian communities all around the Mediterranean Sea. Christianity had also reached parts of northern Europe along the routes of major rivers.**

he executed thousands of Christians for refusing to give up their faith. He ordered the burning of all Christian texts and the destruction of Christian homes.

## UNDERGROUND MEETINGS

In Rome, Christians often held secret meetings in the catacombs—a series of tunnels under the city that were used as burial places. Christian paintings and altars dating from the fourth century have been found in the Roman catacombs.

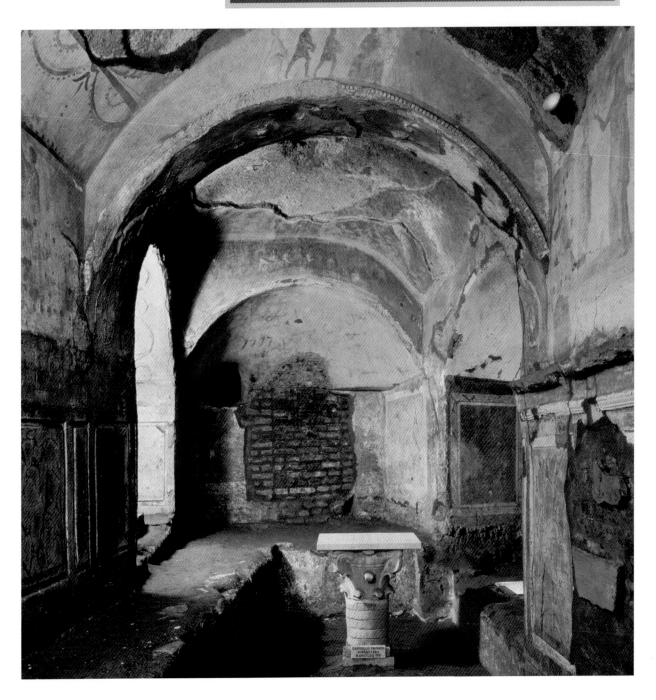

The remains of a catacomb beneath Rome, known as the Catacomb of Priscilla. Some of the catacombs where early Christians met had paintings of Jesus on their walls.

A map of Constantine's empire at its greatest extent. Under Constantine, the Roman Empire became a safe place for Christians to live.

## Bishops, deacons, and priests

In spite of the persecutions, Christianity continued to grow. By the start of the second century, the Christian communities had begun to organize themselves. Groups of Christians built churches where they met regularly for simple services. Each major city had its own bishop. The bishops were the Christian leaders of the surrounding areas. They were helped by deacons and priests. The deacons took care of practical matters, such as helping the poor, while the priests traveled from church to church, leading services.

To keep the Christian world united, the bishops communicated with each other as much as possible. In the third century, the leading bishops were based in Rome, Antioch, and Alexandria, which is in Egypt.

## Constantine and the Christians

Emperor Diocletian died in 305, and the following year, a new and ambitious ruler named Constantine came to power. At this stage in its history, the Roman Empire was divided. Constantine shared control of the Western Empire with Maxentius, while two other rulers controlled the Eastern Empire.

In 312, Constantine fought Maxentius at the Battle of Milvian Bridge, near Rome. Just before the battle, Constantine had a vision. He saw a cross of light in the sky and heard a voice saying, "Conquer by this sign." Constantine immediately ordered all his soldiers to paint the Christian Chi-Rho symbol on their shields. His army was victorious, and Constantine was convinced that he should support the Christians throughout his empire.

## The Edict of Milan

In 313, after his victory over Maxentius, Constantine announced that Christians throughout the Western Empire were free to follow their religion. This famous announcement is known as the Edict of Milan. Constantine also gave money to the bishops to build large churches, known as basilicas, including the splendid basilica of St. Peter in Rome. Constantine announced that Sunday should be a day of rest, and he paid for new copies of the scriptures to be made.

In 324, Constantine defeated the rulers of the Eastern Empire and took control of the entire Roman

Empire. Three years later, he moved his capital from Rome to the city of Byzantium (present-day Istanbul), which he renamed Constantinople. Constantine established Constantinople as a Christian city, with many fine churches.

## The Council of Nicaea
During Constantine's rule, a violent argument broke out between two Christian thinkers. Arius, an Egyptian priest, claimed that Jesus Christ was created by God the Father. But Athanasius, the bishop of Alexandria, said that Christ was part of God and had existed from the beginning of time. This argument threatened to split the church, so Constantine took action. He summoned all the bishops in the empire to a meeting at Nicaea (in present-day Turkey). At the Council of Nicaea in 325, the bishops decided to support Athanasius. They created a statement of their beliefs, which later became known as the Nicene Creed. This creed is still recited today. It states that God the Son is "of one substance with the Father."

### CHRISTIAN SIGNS

The early Christians used secret signs to show that they shared the same faith. These symbols included a fish, an anchor, and a dove. The symbol that Constantine chose to paint on his soldiers' shields was the Chi-Rho sign. It is composed of the first two letters of the word "Christ" in Greek.

**This Roman coin shows the Emperor Constantine wearing a crown of olive leaves. It was made in France around 306.**

## SAINT AUGUSTINE OF HIPPO

St. Augustine was bishop of Hippo in North Africa from 396 to 430. He was a great thinker, who wrote many books on the Christian faith. In particular, Augustine explained that sinners may be forgiven through God's grace. Augustine's ideas had a great effect on Christian teaching. He is known as one of the Fathers of the Church. Augustine witnessed the collapse of the Roman Empire and wrote a famous book called *The City of God*. In it, he stressed the importance of a united Christian community, which was separate from the state.

**A detail from an Italian painting of Saint Augustine.**

**A state religion** About 25 years after Constantine's death, the emperor Julian tried to bring back the Roman gods and goddesses, but it was too late to stop the growth of Christianity. All the emperors after Julian supported the Christians, and in 391, the emperor Theodosius declared that Christianity was the empire's official religion. By this time, the Christian church had become wealthy and powerful. Christians built grand churches and held elaborate services with chanting and singing.

**Rome takes control** During the fourth century, the bishops held several councils to establish the format of worship services and to fix the calendar dates for the Christian festivals. At these councils, the bishop of Rome played a leading role. Gradually, the bishop of Rome became the head of the church, and gained a new title, "pope."

**Hermits, monks, and nuns** Some Christians chose to spend their lives as hermits, living alone in caves in the desert. One famous hermit, St.

Simeon Stylites, spent 30 years sitting on top of a pillar! But not everyone wanted to live as a hermit. In the fourth century, groups of men and women began to form religious communities, though still separated from the rest of society. Male communities were called monasteries, and men living there were called monks. Female communities were called convents, and the women were known as nuns.

**The fall of the Roman Empire** By the 350s, the Roman Empire was under threat from barbarian tribes. These were large groups of fierce warriors, most of them pagans who worshipped their own gods. In 401, an army of Visigoths attacked the city of Milan in northern Italy, and in 410, they invaded Rome. While the Romans fought back in Rome, hordes of Vandals and other tribes were pouring into Germany and France. In 409, the Vandals invaded Spain, and 20 years later, they conquered North Africa. From here, the Vandals moved into Italy, and in 455, they spent 12 days looting Rome. The Roman Empire in the west finally collapsed in 476. This was a major blow for Christianity.

**A map of the Roman Empire showing the routes taken by barbarian invaders. The empire in the west collapsed in 476, but the Eastern Empire, with its capital in Constantinople, resisted the invasions and survived for another one thousand years.**

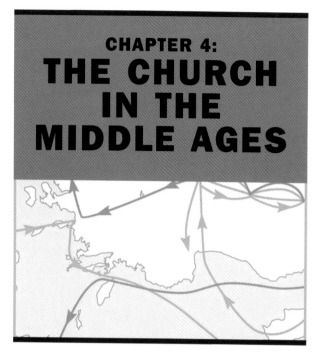

# CHAPTER 4:
# THE CHURCH IN THE MIDDLE AGES

After the fall of Rome in 476, the Western Empire split into small barbarian kingdoms. In many parts of Europe, Christianity died out completely, but the church survived in Rome. Some monasteries also survived, and monks kept Christian learning alive by transcribing holy texts by hand.

**Spreading the message** Gradually, Christian monks in the west began to spread their faith throughout Europe. One of the first areas to be converted to Christianity was Ireland. In the first half of the fifth century, St. Patrick set up Christian monasteries in many parts of Ireland. These monasteries provided a base for other missionaries, who took the Christian message to Britain and France.

In 596, Pope Gregory the Great sent a monk named Augustine to preach to the Angles in southern England.

Mainly Roman Catholics
Mainly Orthodox Christians
Mainly Muslims

A map showing the churches of the east and west after the split in 1054. The map also shows the extent of Islam at this time.

Two centuries later, the English monk St. Boniface converted the tribes of present-day Germany. The Viking people of Scandinavia took longer to accept Christianity, but by the eleventh century, there were churches in Denmark, Sweden, and Norway.

## The eastern church

While the church in the west was slowly rebuilding itself, the church in the eastern part of the Roman Empire was thriving. The capital of the Eastern—or Byzantine—Empire was Constantinople, and this became a very important center for Christianity. In the ninth century, the missionaries St. Cyril and St. Methodius took the Christian message to the Slavs in eastern Europe, and in 988, Prince Vladimir of Russia declared that all Russians should be baptized as Christians.

## The Middle East

Christianity spread through Syria and Persia, but many Christians in these areas rebelled against the standard teachings of the church. In Syria, the rebels were known as Monophysites, and in Persia, they were called Nestorians. Neither of these groups were recognized by the church leaders.

In the seventh century, the new religion of Islam was established in Arabia. Within one hundred years, Islam was widespread, reaching large areas of the Middle East, as well as North Africa and southern Spain. A few Christian communities survived in these areas, but Christians were greatly outnumbered by Muslims (followers of Islam).

## The East–West split

Gradually, the church in the east became increasingly independent from the western church, and after many quarrels, the two factions decided to split in 1054. The eastern church was led by the patriarch in Constantinople, while the western church was led by the pope in Rome. Later, the eastern church became known as the Orthodox Church, and the western church came to be called the Roman Catholic Church.

### CHRISTIANITY IN ETHIOPIA

In the fourth century, a Christian missionary named Frumentius was shipwrecked off the coast of Ethiopia in North Africa. He converted the king of the ancient Ethiopian kingdom of Aksum to Christianity. Two centuries later, the area that is now Sudan also became Christian. Even after North Africa was conquered by Muslim rulers, Ethiopia remained a largely Christian kingdom (see map on page 37).

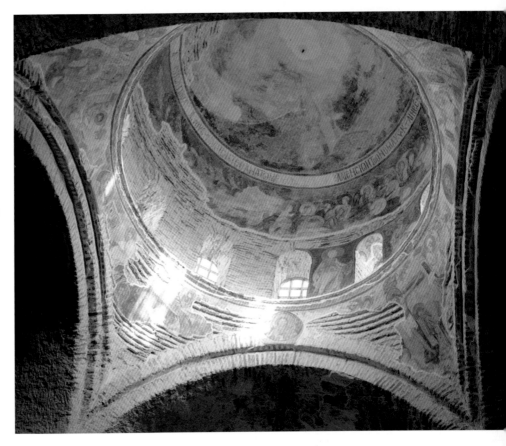

The city of Constantinople (later named Istanbul) was the heart of the eastern church and was full of magnificent church buildings. This photograph shows the dome of the Church of Hagia Sophia in Istanbul.

This map shows some of the most important Christian monasteries in the Middle Ages. It also shows the places where religious orders were founded.

## The growth of the monasteries

During the fourth and fifth centuries, the monasteries became more organized. This was especially due to two men—St. Basil in the east and St. Benedict in the west.

## Saint Benedict's rule

St. Benedict was born in northern Italy in 480. He began his religious life as a hermit, but he soon decided it was best for monks to live together in a community. He established a famous monastery at Monte Cassino and wrote a set of guidelines for his monks to follow.

According to St. Benedict's rule, monks should divide their time between prayer, study, and hard physical work, such as farming. He taught his followers to gather for worship at regular times of day. He also stated that monks should eat plain food, wear simple clothes, called habits, and look after the sick and the poor. After Benedict's death, Benedictine monasteries were established all over western Europe.

## Cluniacs and Cistercians

In the tenth century, Abbot Odilo became the new head of the Benedictine monastery of Cluny in central France. He established a new kind of monastery that concentrated on learning, music, and art. Cluniac monasteries soon spread all over France. Their buildings were beautifully decorated, and the Cluniac monks held elaborate services. However, another French abbot, St. Bernard of Clairvaux, rejected the wealth of the Cluniac monasteries. He established a new order of monks, known as the Cistercians, who led a simple life of prayer and lived in modest buildings. The Cistercian movement was very popular in the twelfth and thirteenth centuries.

## Franciscans and Dominicans

In the early thirteenth century, new religious orders were founded. These were orders of friars, who lived simple lives like monks, but who spent most of their time traveling, preaching, and caring for the poor and sick.

Two men were responsible for the establishment of the friars: St. Dominic and St. Francis. Dominic was a Spanish missionary who worked for the Catholic Church, trying to convert heretics—people who held beliefs that contradicted Catholic teachings. In 1215, Dominic founded an order that would specialize in teaching; these teachers later became known as Dominicans. The first Dominican community was based near Carcassonne in southern France. Later in his life, Dominic also created an order of Dominican nuns.

St. Francis came from the Italian town of Assisi. He led a holy life, teaching and caring for the poor. Francis soon attracted many followers, and in 1209, he established the order of Franciscan friars in Assisi. Three years later, St. Clare, a friend of St. Francis, started the

order of the Poor Clares for women. Like the Franciscans, the Poor Clares lived in simple buildings and spent most of their time helping the poor.

## ORTHODOX MONASTERIES

In the mid-fourth century, St. Basil the Great founded a monastery in Pontus, south of the Black Sea. He wrote a set of rules for his monks, instructing them to pray, carry out good works, help the sick and the poor, and study the Bible. Over the next few centuries, many more monasteries were founded in Turkey and Greece, all of them following St. Basil's rules.

A medieval painting showing St. Benedict giving his blessing to the members of his order.

Supporters of the pope in Avignon
Supporters of the pope in Rome
Changing support

0     250km
0     250 miles

**A map of medieval Europe, showing the followers of the rival popes based in Avignon and Rome. The Holy Roman emperors shifted their allegience, sometimes supporting one pope, sometimes the other.**

### Church and state

The pope was the head of the western church, but he also had to rely on the help of secular (nonreligious) rulers, such as kings and emperors. During the Middle Ages, there were times when the popes and rulers supported each other. However, there were often dramatic power struggles.

### Charlemagne's empire

One of the Roman Catholic Church's great early supporters was the emperor Charlemagne. He became leader of the Franks in 768 and built a large Christian empire, which covered most of present-day Germany and France. In 800, Pope Leo III crowned Charlemagne emperor of the Romans, and Charlemagne promised to support the church. This alliance with Charlemagne gave the Roman Catholic Church a great deal of power. However, after Charlemagne's death, his empire collapsed.

### The Holy Roman Empire

In 955, the German leader Otto I gained control of large parts of central and eastern Europe. The pope granted Otto and his descendants the title of Holy Roman Emperor. This title gave the emperors control over all the bishops in their lands, and they used the bishops to help them rule.

However, the popes wanted to control the bishops themselves, and they hoped to gain money from the bishops' lands. During the Middle Ages, the popes and emperors had many fierce quarrels over their rights to control the bishops and their lands.

**Popes in France** In 1309, two men competed for the title of pope. One of them appealed to the French king for help and moved to Avignon in southern France, while the rival pope stayed in Rome. For the next 100 years, the official popes were based in France, and for part of this time, rival popes ruled in Rome.

Some countries in western Europe followed the Avignon pope, while others supported the pope in Rome (see map on page 24). The situation was made

even more complicated because the Holy Roman emperors often changed sides. This major split in the church was called the Great Schism. It significantly weakened the power of the Roman Catholic popes and bishops.

## PILGRIMAGES

During the Middle Ages, many Christians went on pilgrimages. They traveled long distances to holy shrines, where saints were buried or sacred objects were kept. Pilgrims made these journeys hoping that God would forgive their sins and cure their diseases.

Many people made a pilgrimage to Jerusalem or Rome. In England, pilgrims visited the shrine of St. Thomas à Becket in Canterbury. St. Thomas was an archbishop who fought with King Henry II and was murdered by the king's knights.

This painting of English pilgrims comes from an illustrated version of *The Canterbury Tales* by Geoffrey Chaucer. *The Canterbury Tales*, written in the fourteenth century, follows a group of pilgrims making a pilgrimage from London to Canterbury and telling stories along the way.

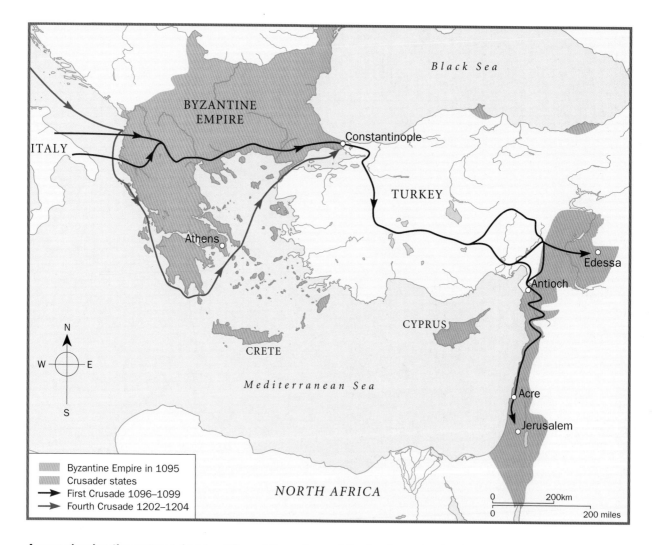

**A map showing the routes taken by different Crusades and the land won by the Crusaders.**

### Muslims and Christians

By the end of the eleventh century, many Christians were focused on the Holy Land. For 400 years, Palestine had been ruled by Muslim Turks, and for most of that time, the Turks had allowed Christian pilgrims to travel to Jerusalem. However, by the 1090s, relations between Turks and Christians had become much worse, and some pilgrims had been attacked.

Christians in the eastern church felt especially threatened by the Turks. The Turkish lands lay next to the Christian Byzantine Empire, and the Turks were gradually taking over Byzantine lands. This alarmed Christians in both the eastern and western churches.

### The Crusades begin

In 1095, Pope Urban II preached a sermon, urging all Christians to go on a "holy war," or Crusade, to drive the Muslims out of the Holy Land. Nobles from France, Germany, and Italy gathered their armies and set off on the long journey to the Middle East. This was the start of the First Crusade.

In 1099, the Crusaders captured Jerusalem and the surrounding lands. Some Crusaders stayed to defend their newly conquered territory, but many others returned home. In 1144, a Muslim army seized the city of Edessa (Urfa, in present-day Turkey), and the Second Crusade failed to win it back. In 1187, the Muslims, led by Saladin, recaptured Jerusalem.

### Later Crusades

The Third Crusade was led by the rulers of France, England, and Germany. They won many battles and captured the city of Acre, but they did not succeed in winning back Jerusalem.

## CRUSADER KNIGHTS

During the Crusades, some new orders of warrior monks were formed, known as Crusader knights. These men lived like monks, dedicating their lives to God, but they were also fierce warriors. The main orders of Crusader knights were the Knights Templar, the Knights Hospitaller, and the Teutonic Knights.

**A medieval artist's impression of the capture of the city of Antioch. The Crusaders won Antioch from the Muslim Turks during the First Crusade.**

The Fourth Crusade only reached as far as Constantinople. Here, the Crusaders turned on the Byzantines and took over their city. Crusaders from western Europe ruled Constantinople for the next 60 years and sent many Byzantine treasures back home. This shameful period created deep divisions between the eastern and western churches.

During the next 100 years, there were three more Crusades, but the Christians did not win any major new lands. In 1229, the Muslims agreed to return Jerusalem to the Christians, but this agreement did not last. In 1244, a Muslim army recaptured Jerusalem, and in 1291, the Muslims finally conquered Acre, the last city held by the Crusaders, marking the end of the Crusades.

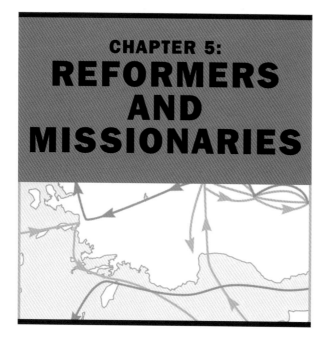

# CHAPTER 5: REFORMERS AND MISSIONARIES

**Problems in the Church** By the early 1500s, many people in western Europe were unhappy with the Roman Catholic Church. Many church leaders seemed to be interested only in wealth and power, and people complained that their local priests were poorly educated and lazy. In particular, people blamed the church for the sale of indulgences—pardons for people's sins. Wealthy people paid large sums of money for these indulgences, while the poor could not afford to have their sins pardoned.

**Martin Luther** In 1517, a German priest named Martin Luther wrote a list of 95 ways in which the Catholic Church could be reformed. He nailed this list to the church door in Wittenberg, Germany, and his ideas soon spread. This made the leaders of the church very angry, and in 1520, the pope excommunicated Luther, banning him from the church forever.

Luther went into hiding and worked on his ideas of how the Catholic Church should be run. He believed that church services should be simple and that people should read the Bible for themselves, rather than being read to by a priest. Luther helped make this possible by translating the New Testament from Greek into German.

Martin Luther had intended to reform the Catholic Church from the inside, but by the 1520s, it was clear that

In the early years of the sixteenth century, determined individuals began to publicly protest against the Roman Catholic Church. At first, these protesters simply wished to reform the church, but instead, their protests led to the creation of entirely new Christian groups. The dramatic reshaping of the western church in the sixteenth century is known as the Reformation, and the members of the new churches became known as Protestants or Nonconformists.

**One of the earliest copies of Luther's Bible, translated from Greek into German. This copy was owned by Luther himself and includes notes and corrections made by him.**

## A PLAINER STYLE

Protestant churches are generally much less ornate than Roman Catholic churches. Unlike Catholic churches, Protestant churches do not have any statues of the Virgin Mary or the saints, because Protestants believe that they should communicate directly with God and Jesus, rather than praying to Mary and the saints. The one Protestant exception to this practice is the Anglican Church, a Protestant Church that uses many Roman Catholic buildings (see pages 30–31). Anglican churches often have statues of saints.

**A map of Europe showing the location of the major printing presses in the fifteenth and sixteenth centuries.**

this was impossible. Gradually, people all over Germany began to hold simple services based on Luther's ideas, and the Lutheran Church was established. By the 1550s, Lutheranism had spread to Denmark, Norway, and Sweden. Other Protestant churches followed the Lutherans' example and held simple services with readings from the Bible and the singing of hymns.

## The printing press

The advent of mechanized printing played a key role in the rapid spread of Luther's ideas. In 1436, the German Johannes Gutenberg invented the printing press, and by 1500, there were printing presses all over Europe, especially in Germany. Luther was a gifted and popular writer who wrote many pamphlets that were printed and widely circulated. Because of the printing press, ordinary people could read Luther's translation of the Bible.

**Calvinism** John Calvin was a French priest who broke away from the Roman Catholic Church. In 1541, he established a group of Protestants in Geneva, Switzerland. Like Luther, Calvin emphasized the importance of the Bible in Christian worship. He also claimed that some chosen people would be saved and go to heaven, while others would go to hell. Calvin wrote several books on the Bible, which were widely read in Europe. Calvinism was very popular in Switzerland, and it also spread to Scotland and the Netherlands.

**Henry VIII's rebellion** The English Protestant revolt began when King Henry VIII fought with the pope. Henry wanted to divorce his first wife, Catherine of Aragon, and marry his mistress, Anne Boleyn. But the pope refused to grant him a divorce. This made Henry so angry that he decided to break away from the Catholic Church. In an act of Parliament of 1534, Henry was named supreme head of the Church of England. This was the start of the Anglican Church.

Mainly Anglican
Mainly Lutheran
Mainly Calvinist
Mainly Catholic
Mixed Lutheran and Calvinist
Mainly Orthodox Christian

**A map of religious groups in Europe around 1560, at the end of the Reformation.**

**One of the many ruined monasteries is Rievaulx Abbey in Yorkshire, England. The dissolution of the monasteries by Henry VIII led to many grand buildings falling into ruin.**

In some ways, the Anglican Church continued the practices of the Roman Catholic Church. It still had bishops and parish priests and it took over all the Catholic cathedrals and churches. However, there were some differences. Bibles were placed in Anglican churches for the public to read, and services were held in English, not in Latin. In 1549, the Archbishop of Canterbury, Thomas Cranmer, produced the Book of Common Prayer, which outlined all the services of the Anglican Church. Today, Anglicans around the world use prayer books based on Cranmer's original work.

In 1538, Henry VIII began a campaign of dissolving, or closing down, the Catholic monasteries in his kingdom. It was well known that many monks and nuns did not lead holy lives, but Henry also wanted to destroy the power and wealth of the Catholic Church in England. Some of the monastery buildings were sold to wealthy nobles, but many others fell into ruin.

## THE PRESBYTERIAN CHURCH

The Presbyterian Church began in Scotland in the 1560s. It was founded by John Knox, who had spent several years as a preacher at a Calvinist church in Geneva, Switzerland. In the Presbyterian Church, there is no fixed form of worship, and each congregation is governed by a group of presbyters, or elders, who are all of equal rank.

When James I became king of England in 1603, he recognized Presbyterianism as the national faith in Scotland. Presbyterianism later spread to England, Wales, Ireland, and North America.

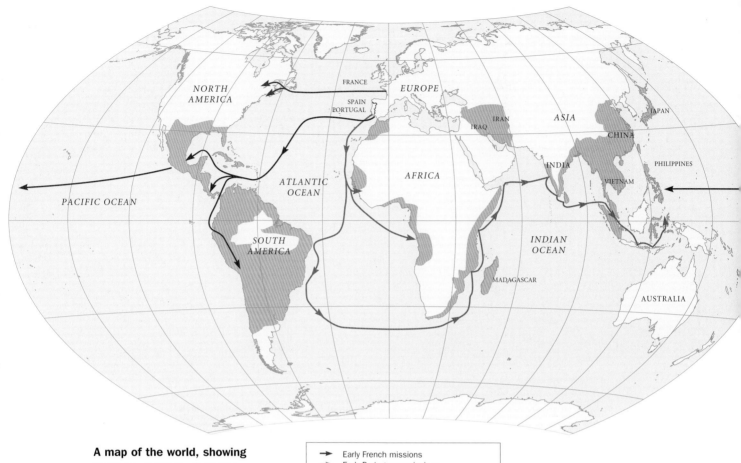

**A map of the world, showing journeys made by Catholic missionaries between the sixteenth and eighteenth centuries.**

→ Early French missions
→ Early Portuguese missions
→ Early Spanish missions
▨ Areas with established churches by 1750

### The Counter-Reformation
As the Reformation gathered strength, the Roman Catholic leaders tried to win people back to their church. They began a reform movement of their own, which became known as the Counter-Reformation.

Some of the first areas of reform concerned the monasteries. The existing monastic orders were reorganized and several new orders were created. Catholic leaders set up training colleges for priests, built elaborate new cathedrals and churches, and attacked the Protestants in sermons and books. From 1545 to 1563, the leaders of the Church met as a group called the Council of Trent. They used the council to restate their beliefs, condemn Protestant ideas, and plan reforms of the church.

### The Jesuits
The most famous of the new monastic orders was the Society of Jesus, also known as the Jesuit order. It was founded in 1534 by the Spanish monk Ignatius Loyola. Jesuits lived a life of strict discipline and devotion to Christ; they also promised to carry out any task that the pope demanded of them. The Jesuits ran schools and colleges and traveled as missionaries, first to Poland, then to more distant lands.

### Catholic missionaries
Beginning in the early 1500s, Catholic missionaries accompanied conquering armies to newly discovered lands in South America, Africa, and Asia. Jesuit missionaries were especially adventurous. For example, Francis Xavier led missions to India, Ceylon (present-day Sri Lanka), and Japan in the 1540s and 1550s, while Matteo Ricci traveled to China in 1582 and stayed there for the next 20 years.

By the seventeenth century, Catholic missionaries had converted hundreds of thousands of people to Christianity and established churches, monasteries, and schools in many parts of Asia and South America.

However, not all the missions were successful. In the 1640s, a group of French Jesuit missionaries in Canada were killed by Native Americans.

**Religious wars** In many parts of Europe, the clash between Protestants and Catholics led to war. In Germany, Lutherans and Catholics fought each other in the Thirty Years' War from 1618–48, while in France, French Protestants, known as Huguenots, fought the Catholic king and his supporters. The most horrific event during these Wars of Religion was the St. Bartholomew's Day massacre of 1572, when thousands of Huguenots were killed in a single day.

## BAROQUE ART

During the time of the Counter-Reformation, a new style of religious art and architecture developed. This style is known as Baroque. It is very elaborate and was popular with many church leaders because it appealed to people's emotions and encouraged them to be more devout. Baroque painters and sculptors, such as Gian Lorenzo Bernini, produced dramatic images of saints experiencing miraculous visions and martyrs suffering terrible deaths.

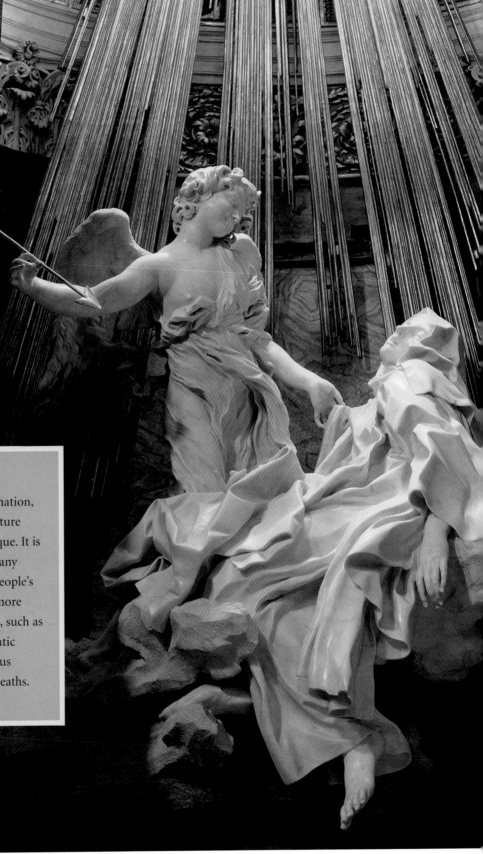

*The Ecstasy of Saint Teresa* was created by Gian Lorenzo Bernini between 1647 and 1652. Works such as this had a powerful effect on Catholic Christians.

## QUAKERS

The Society of Friends—or the Quakers—was founded in England around 1650. Quakers gather in meeting houses rather than churches and they stress the importance of quiet meditation. Soon after The Society of Friends was formed, some Quakers emigrated to North America, but they faced persecution there from larger Christian groups. In the 1670s, a Quaker named William Penn began to purchase land for the Quakers in the area that would later become Pennsylvania. Today, a number of Quaker organizations have their headquarters in Pennsylvania.

**Puritans** The Puritan movement developed in England in the sixteenth century, when some Protestants became unhappy with the Anglican Church under Queen Elizabeth I (1558–1603). The Puritans disapproved of displays of wealth and ceremony. They dressed plainly and followed a simple form of worship.

By the 1650s, the Puritans had gained political power in England. In the previous decade, there had been a power struggle between the English king, Charles I, and Parliament, the law-making assembly. This

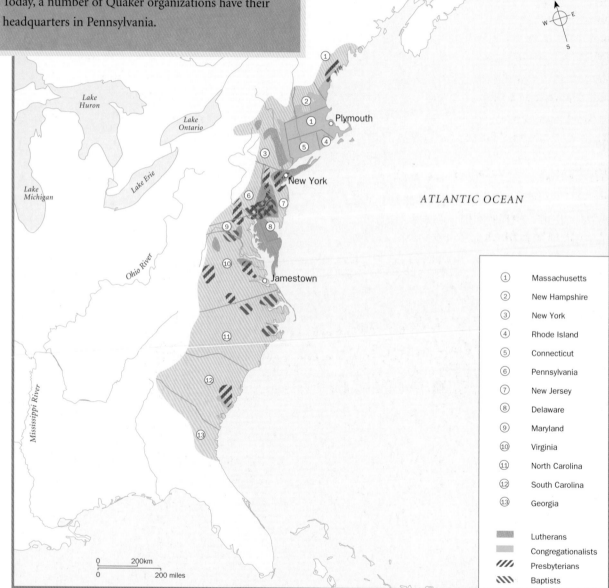

| | |
|---|---|
| ① | Massachusetts |
| ② | New Hampshire |
| ③ | New York |
| ④ | Rhode Island |
| ⑤ | Connecticut |
| ⑥ | Pennsylvania |
| ⑦ | New Jersey |
| ⑧ | Delaware |
| ⑨ | Maryland |
| ⑩ | Virginia |
| ⑪ | North Carolina |
| ⑫ | South Carolina |
| ⑬ | Georgia |

Lutherans
Congregationalists
Presbyterians
Baptists

**A map of the North American colonies in 1750, showing the main Christian groups. The Lutheran and Congregationalist Churches had a strong following, but no single religious group dominated the colonies.**

struggle led to a civil war from 1642–49. Parliament's forces were triumphant, and one of their leaders, Oliver Cromwell, took power. Cromwell was a Puritan, and from 1653–58, he ruled England according to Puritan principles. He closed many ale houses and discouraged dancing and theatergoing. However, in 1660, the son of Charles I, Charles II, became king and restored Anglicanism as the official religion of England.

**Baptists** Like the Puritans, the Baptists were a breakaway group from the Anglican Church. Originally known as Separatists, they were persecuted in England and escaped to Holland in 1608. The Separatists returned to England in 1612 and attracted many followers. By the following century, the Baptist Church was well established in Europe and America. Baptists only baptize adult believers, because Christ was not baptized until he was an adult. In the Baptist Church, baptism is performed by total immersion in water.

**Christians in North America** In 1620, a group of Puritans and Separatists, known as Pilgrims, sailed from England to North America. They arrived in Plymouth, Massachusetts, on the east coast of the

continent, and established a colony there. Over the next century, Protestants from England, Scotland, Germany, and the Netherlands all made the journey to North America. Most of them settled in the eastern and northern regions of the continent, and these areas became predominantly Protestant.

In other parts of North America, the Catholic religion was dominant. The French owned large amounts of land in the center of the continent, until it was sold to the United States in the nineteenth century. Beginning in the 1500s, the Spanish settled in the western part of America; Roman Catholicism was the main religion of the Spanish settlers.

**The First Great Awakening** In the 1730s, a young church minister named Jonathan Edwards traveled along the eastern coast of the U.S., preaching with great passion. Edwards's sermons had a dramatic effect on his listeners and won thousands of converts to Christianity. Edwards's followers built new churches all over New England, and he inspired many other preachers to spread the word. This movement later became known as the First Great Awakening.

Once the Pilgrims had settled in Plymouth, they held a service of thanksgiving to God. This painting shows the first sermon delivered in Plymouth.

## CHAPTER 6: INTO THE MODERN WORLD

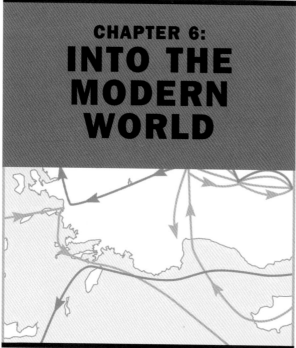

In the eighteenth century, Christian preachers moved from place to place, spreading their message of salvation. They held open-air meetings where they preached and encouraged people to pray and sing hymns together. This type of worship, in which the Christian message is taken into the wider world, is often known as evangelism. One of the first evangelist Christians was John Wesley, who founded Methodism.

### John Wesley and the Methodists

John Wesley trained as an Anglican minister, but in 1738, he experienced a dramatic conversion and began to spread the message that Christians could be saved from their sins. At first, he preached his message in Anglican churches, but later, he traveled around the country holding outdoor meetings wherever he went.

Methodists conduct simple services that include singing rousing hymns and preaching passionate

### THE SALVATION ARMY

In 1861, the Methodist minister William Booth and his wife, Catherine, began a Christian mission to help the poor in the East End of London. To carry out this work, Booth established an organization called the Salvation Army. Booth's army of men and women dressed in easily recognizable uniforms and held lively street services, attracting large crowds with their cheerful band music. In addition to teaching the gospel, the Salvation Army offered shelter and food to people in need. By 1912, the army had branches in more than 50 countries.

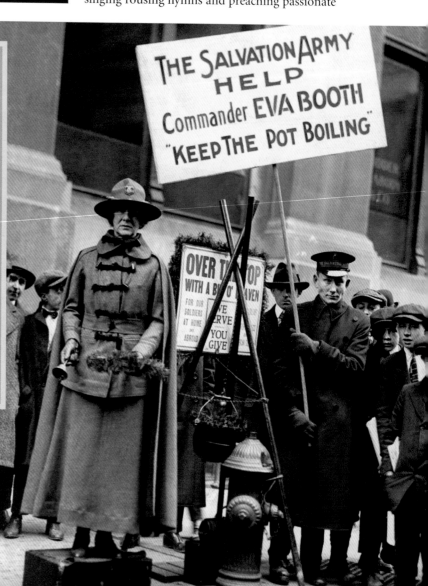

**Evangeline Booth, the daughter of William and Catherine Booth, was one of the leaders of the Salvation Army for many years. She is shown here raising money for the Salvation Army.**

sermons. Methodists strive to live a virtuous life and help the poor. John Wesley made sure that the Methodist Church was well organized, and used traveling preachers to spread the word. His movement grew rapidly in the U.S. and the United Kingdom.

## The Second Great Awakening

Around the end of the eighteenth century, a powerful new wave of religious feeling swept through the U.S. Known as the Second Great Awakening, it started with "camp meetings" held in tents in Kentucky and Tennessee. People stayed for days in the camps, listening to fiery sermons and being baptized by the thousands in local rivers. Later, this Christian revival spread to the East Coast, where powerful preachers such as Lyman Beecher and Charles Finney drew enormous crowds.

Many of the newly converted Christians worked to change American society. In particular, the Second Great Awakening led many people to campaign against slavery.

## New religious groups

During the nineteenth century, several new sects, or branches, of Christianity were founded in the U.S., usually by someone who preached a new "revelation" of the Bible's message. Some of the most successful sects were the Mormons, the Christian Scientists, and the Jehovah's Witness movement. These three religious groups soon gained large numbers of followers around the world.

## Christian missionaries

By the 1850s, countries such as the UK, Germany, and France had developed large colonies in Africa and Asia. Christians were determined to spread their faith to these areas, and

**A map of Africa in 1914, showing all the areas reached by Christian missionaries. The map also shows the ancient Christian community of Ethiopia.**

Missionary activity by 1914
Ethiopian Church (founded 4th century)
Mainly Muslim area

by 1900, Christian missionaries had established churches in almost every country in the world.

Christian missionaries often did more than build churches and teach Christianity. They also set up hospitals and schools and introduced new farming methods. A major part of missionary work was providing people with copies of the Bible in their own language, so they could read it for themselves. By 1900, the New Testament had been translated into more than 500 languages.

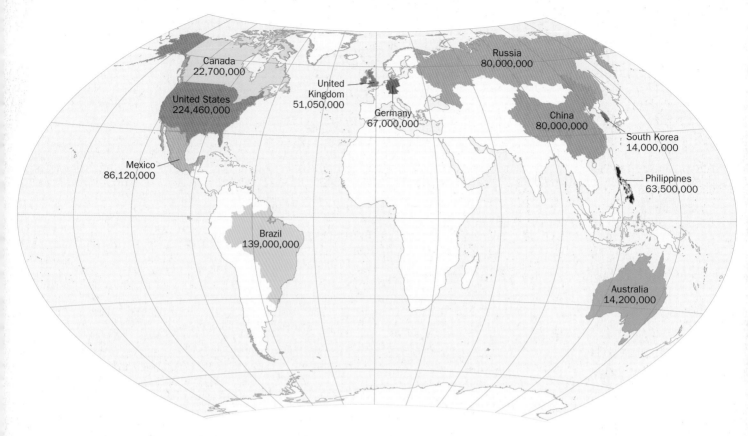

A map of the world ca. 2000, showing countries with a significant proportion of Christians. The map provides the approximate number of Christians in these countries.

**The Charismatic movement** Around the start of the twentieth century, a new Christian movement, known as the Pentecostal Church, began in Los Angeles, California. Pentecostal Christians are often known as Charismatic Christians, or simply Charismatics. They hold lively services in which everyone enthusiastically participates; some Charismatics claim to have gifts of prophecy and healing.

By the 1950s, the Charismatic movement had spread throughout the world. In 2000, the movement had an estimated 500 million members, making it the fastest-growing Christian movement worldwide. Today, it is especially popular in South America.

## THE ORTHODOX CHURCH

After the Orthodox Church split from the Roman Catholic Church in 1054, it followed a very different path from the church in the West. In 1453, Constantinople was conquered by Muslim Turks, and the church in Turkey and the Middle East struggled to survive. However, in Greece and Russia, the Orthodox Church continued to thrive, although the Russians and Greeks developed different traditions.

In 1922, Russia formed a Communist state called the Soviet Union. The Soviet leaders saw Christianity as a major threat to their system of government. Within a few years, more than a thousand bishops and priests had been executed and hundreds of monasteries had been destroyed. Persecution of Christians continued until the collapse of the Soviet Union in 1991. Since then, the church in Russia has experienced a dramatic revival.

The American evangelist Billy Graham has brought the Christian message to millions of people. He is shown here preaching in New York.

## Modern evangelism

In the 1950s, there was a new surge in evangelism, as people spread the Christian message through exciting sermons and rousing hymns. Evangelism was especially popular in the U.S., where it was greatly helped by the emergence of television as a medium of mass communication.

The leading evangelist of the twentieth century was the American preacher Billy Graham. He has traveled around the world many times, speaking to an estimated 210 million people in 185 countries.

## Televangelists

Over the last 20 years, there have been a growing number of "televangelists" who spread their message through television. In addition to conducting televised services, some televangelists also provide commentary on current events. In the U.S., there are several television channels devoted entirely to programs with a Christian message.

## Liberation theology

In the 1970s, a new movement began within the Roman Catholic Church in South America known as liberation theology. It is based on the idea that Christians have a duty to help the poor and the suffering. Followers of liberation theology believe that they should defend their people against systems of government that favor the rich and powerful at the expense of the poor. Some priests in South America have made a stand against corrupt governments, and a few have been killed. For example, Archbishop Oscar Romero of El Salvador was murdered in 1980 for standing up for the rights of the poor in his country.

# CHRISTIANITY

### Christianity today
At the start of the twenty-first century, Christianity is the world's largest religion. More than a third of the world's population describe themselves as Christians. With more than two billion Christians worldwide, Christianity has almost twice as many followers as Islam, the world's second largest faith.

### Different patterns
In Africa, much of Asia, and parts of South America, Christianity is growing very fast. But in Europe, the Christian religion is in decline. Attendance at church services in Europe fell dramatically in the second half of the twentieth century, and now only 10 percent of Europeans are regular churchgoers. However, in the U.S., Christianity is still very popular. A majority of Americans describe themselves as Christians, and up to 40 percent of the population attends church regularly.

### Fundamentalism
The Christian Fundamentalist movement began in the U.S. in the early twentieth century as a reaction to the lack of faith in modern society. Since then, it has grown significantly, mainly in the U.S.

Fundamentalist Christians adhere to the basics—or fundamentals—of their religion and emphasize the importance of belief in the literal truth of the Bible. They also campaign for strict moral standards in public and private life. Many Fundamentalists believe that God created the world in seven days, as described in the Bible. These "creationists" reject the theory of evolution, which states that the world as we know it evolved throughout millions of years.

### Women priests
By the end of the twentieth century, several Christian groups decided to ordain women as priests or ministers. The Danish Lutherans led the way when they elected their first female priest in 1947. American Methodists and Presbyterians began ordaining women in 1956. In 1988, the American Episcopalian Church—the American branch of the Anglican Church—elected its first woman bishop. The Anglicans in the UK approved the ordination of women priests in 1994. However, there is still resistance to the idea of female priests in the Roman Catholic and Orthodox Churches.

**Christianity is thriving in many parts of Asia. In 2004, around 100,000 South Koreans held a prayer meeting in a soccer stadium to celebrate Easter.**

**A map showing the location of the majority of Christians compared to people of other world faiths.**

| | |
|---|---|
| ▨ | Buddhism |
| ▨ | Christianity |
| ▨ | Hinduism |
| ▨ | Indigenous Religions |
| ▨ | Islam |
| ▨ | Judaism |
| ▨ | Nonreligious |
| ▨ | Sikhism |

## Coming together

In recent years, the different denominations—or branches—of Christianity have made a greater effort to understand each other and even work together. These efforts to encourage cooperation are known as the ecumenical movement. In 1948, the World Council of Churches was established to encourage the ecumenical spirit. On a smaller scale, there are many shared activities between different denominations in local communities.

In 1964, Pope Paul VI visited Patriarch Athenagoras in Istanbul. This was the first major attempt to heal the division between the Roman Catholic and Orthodox Churches since their split in 1054. Since this visit, there have been more meetings between popes and patriarchs.

One outstanding example of the ecumenical spirit is the Taizé community. This Christian community was founded by a Swiss monk, Brother Roger, in the French town of Taizé, near Lyons. The Taizé brothers hold simple services that can be shared by people of all denominations. Every year, thousands of people flock to Taizé to worship together.

## GIVING AID

Some Christians see it as their duty to help the many people in the world who are suffering from poverty, hunger, and disease. Christian charities, such as Christian Aid, send money and support to people who are suffering, and numerous Christians devote their lives to helping others. In many parts of the world, Christians have set up hospitals and caring communities, which are often run by monks and nuns. The most famous of these nuns is Mother Teresa, who devoted her life to helping the poor and homeless in India (see page 43).

# GREAT LIVES

## Jesus (ca. 4–33 CE)

Jesus was born in Bethlehem in the Roman province of Judaea and spent his childhood in Nazareth, in northern Palestine. After his baptism by John the Baptist, Jesus began his adult work of preaching, performing miracles, and healing the sick. He invited 12 disciples to help him in his work, and everywhere he went, he gained more followers. Jesus spent most of his adult life in the area of Galilee, in northern Palestine. In the final weeks of his life, he traveled to Jerusalem, where he was arrested, tried, and sentenced to death by crucifixion. Christians believe that Jesus rose from the dead three days after his death.

## St. Paul (ca. 3–68 CE)

Paul was originally named Saul. He was born in Tarsus (in present-day Turkey) and was the son of a Pharisee—a high-ranking Jewish priest. According to the Bible, Saul was converted to Christianity on the road to Damascus, and after his conversion, he changed his name to Paul. He made a series of great missionary journeys throughout Syria, Turkey, and Greece, and he founded many Christian communities. Paul was eventually arrested in Jerusalem and sent to Rome for trial. In Rome, he was kept as a prisoner inside his house, but during this time, he wrote many letters to the communities he had founded. These letters were later included in the New Testament. Nobody knows how Paul died, but he may have been put to death by the Roman emperor, Nero.

## St. Benedict (ca. 480–547)

St. Benedict was the son of an Italian nobleman. He was educated in Rome, but as a teenager, he rejected the worldly life and lived as a hermit. Gradually, Benedict's fame spread, and people joined him. He built 12 monastic houses for his followers and encouraged them to live a simple life, dividing their time between hard physical work, study, and prayer. After a few years, Benedict set up a second community in the mountain village of Monte Cassino. Benedict spent the rest of his life there, and during this time, wrote his famous rules, providing guidelines on how monks should live.

## St. Francis of Assisi (1182–1226)

St. Francis was born in Assisi in northern Italy as the son of a rich merchant. When he was around 24 years old, Francis gave up all his possessions and lived the life of a poor man, wandering the countryside and preaching the Christian message. He attracted many followers and created a community of "brothers" who lived a simple life like him. Later, the brothers became known as friars. Francis was famous for the kindness and gentleness he showed to both people and animals. He went on several journeys, and everywhere he went, he preached and cared for the poor.

## Martin Luther (1483–1546)

Martin Luther was a brilliant scholar who also became a university teacher and a preacher. However, Luther grew increasingly unhappy about the corruption in the Catholic Church. In 1517, he wrote a proposition called *Ninety-five Theses*, outlining all of the problems in the Catholic Church, and posted them on a church door in Wittenberg, Germany. In 1520, the pope wrote a document condemning Luther's arguments that Luther burned in public. Luther was excommunicated and the Catholic Church threatened to burn him as a heretic. He went into hiding and worked on his ideas for a new kind of church. Luther also translated the New Testament into German. He eventually returned to Wittenberg and spent the rest of his life preaching and spreading his ideas.

## John Wesley (1703–91)

John Wesley was born in Lincolnshire, UK. He trained to be an Anglican minister at Oxford University. There, he joined a group of young men who were called "Methodists" because they lived according to very strict rules. In 1738, Wesley experienced a "conversion," in which he understood that Christ could save him. From then on, he devoted his life to preaching this message. John and his brother Charles preached in churches, on the streets, and at public meetings. Wesley organized his new Methodist Church, and encouraged the leaders of his church to play an active part in social reforms.

# FURTHER INFORMATION

## Martin Luther King, Jr. (1929–68)

Martin Luther King, Jr. was born in Atlanta, Georgia. The son of a Baptist minister, King also trained as a minister in the Baptist Church. He was a brilliant and moving speaker and he soon became a leading figure in the campaign for civil rights for African Americans. In 1963, King made a famous speech in which he described his dream of a country where everyone was equal. He also helped to organize a march of 200,000 people on Washington, D.C. to demand racial equality. Partly as a result of King's campaigns, the U.S. government passed new civil rights laws in 1964. In 1968, King was assassinated in Memphis, Tennessee.

## Mother Teresa of Calcutta (1910–97)

Mother Teresa was originally named Agnes Gonxha Bojaxhiu. She was born in Macedonia, but at the age of 18, she traveled to Ireland to join a convent of nuns who sent teachers to India. After training for a few months, she went to India and worked as a teacher in a Catholic school in Calcutta. Mother Teresa was a schoolteacher for 17 years, but in 1948, she felt she heard the voice of God urging her to devote her life to helping the poor. She began to care for the poor, the sick, and the dying in Calcutta and set up a school for children who lived in poor urban areas. Many people helped her with her work. In 1950, she founded a new religious order, known as the Missionaries of Charity.

## Archbishop Desmond Tutu (born 1931)

Desmond Tutu was born in the Transvaal region of South Africa. First, he was trained as a teacher. Then in 1960, he was ordained as an Anglican priest. In 1986, Tutu was appointed Archbishop of Cape Town. He was one of the leading figures in the struggle to end apartheid in South Africa, where black people were treated as second-class citizens. After apartheid was abolished in 1994, Archbishop Tutu worked to set up the Truth and Reconciliation Commission so that those who committed injustices in the name of apartheid were given a fair hearing and then granted forgiveness. The commission was recognized as an outstanding example of Christian principles.

## Books

*Christianity* by Philip Wilkinson (DK Children, 2006)

*The Story of Christianity: 2000 Years of Faith* by Michael Collins and Matthew Price (DK Adult, 2003)

*World Beliefs and Cultures: Christianity* by Sue Penney (Heinemann Library, 2001)

## Web sites

www.bbc.co.uk/religion/religions/christianity/
A brief guide to Christianity, including sections on history, customs and holy days as well as news features on Christianity today.

www.justus.anglican.org/resources/bio/
Very brief sketches of the lives of famous Christians.

www.rejesus.co.uk/
A large Web site on the Christian religion, including interviews, prayers, and videos on the life of Christ.

# TIME LINE

ca. 4 CE Birth of Jesus.

ca. 27 Jesus gathers his disciples and begins to teach and perform miracles.

ca. 33 Crucifixion of Jesus.

ca. 35 Conversion of St. Paul.

ca. 46 St. Paul sets off on the first of his three missionary journeys.

64 After the Great Fire of Rome, Emperor Nero begins to persecute Christians.

ca. 65 St. Mark completes his Gospel, the first of the Gospels of the New Testament.

303 Emperor Diocletian begins his great persecution of Christians.

305 The missionary, Frumentius, converts the people of Ethiopia.

312 Emperor Constantine has a vision before the Battle of Milvian Bridge. After the battle, he encourages Christianity in the Roman Empire.

313 Constantine issues the Edict of Milan, allowing Christians in the empire to follow their religion.

325 Constantine holds the Council of Nicaea—the first of the great church councils.

ca. 350 St. Basil establishes a set of rules for monks in the eastern church.

391 Emperor Theodosius makes Christianity the official religion of the Roman Empire.

393 The New Testament is completed.

410 St. Augustine of Hippo begins to write *The City of God*.

ca. 440 St. Patrick converts Irish tribes.

ca. 500 St. Benedict establishes a community of monks. This is the start of the Benedictine order.

597 St. Augustine converts the Angles of southern England.

800 Pope Leo III crowns Charlemagne "emperor of the Romans."

909 The first Cluniac monastery is founded.

988 Russia becomes a Christian country.

1054 The Orthodox and Roman Catholic Churches split.

1095 Pope Urban II calls Christians to go on the First Crusade.

1098 St. Bernard founds the Cistercian order.

1209 St. Francis establishes the first order of Franciscan friars.

1215 St. Dominic establishes a community of monks called the Dominican order.

1309 Pope Clement V moves from Rome to Avignon, France.

1517 Martin Luther posts his *Ninety-five Theses* on the church door in Wittenberg, Germany.

1520 Martin Luther is excommunicated. This leads to Lutheranism.

1534 King Henry VIII announces that he is supreme head of the Church of England. This marks the start of Anglicanism.

St. Ignatius Loyola establishes the Society of Jesus.

1541 John Calvin establishes the Calvinist Church.

1545 The Council of Trent meets. Meetings continue until 1563.

1560s John Knox founds the Presbyterian Church in Scotland.

1612 The Separatists, later known as the Baptists, become established in England.

1618 The Thirty Years' War between Catholics and Protestants begins in Germany.

1620 The Pilgrims establish a colony in North America.

1650s The Society of Friends is formed. Later, the Friends are known as Quakers.

1738 John Wesley preaches a new form of Christianity. This marks the beginning of Methodism.

1861 William Booth founds the Salvation Army.

1900s The Pentecostal, or Charismatic, movement begins in Los Angeles, California.

1948 The World Council of Churches is founded.

1964 The pope and the patriarch meet to heal divisions between the Roman Catholic and Orthodox Churches.

1970s The liberation theology movement begins in South America.

2000 Christians around the world celebrate two thousand years of Christianity.

# FACTS AND FIGURES

## Festivals and seasons

The main festivals and seasons of the Christian year are Advent, Christmas, Lent, and Easter. Some festivals, such as Christmas, are celebrated on the same date every year; others, such as Easter, vary slightly every year.

| Month | Event | What happens |
|---|---|---|
| November/December | Advent | The season of Advent covers the four Sundays before Christmas. During Advent, Christians remember the coming of the Angel Gabriel to Mary and the events leading to the birth of Jesus. |
| December or January | Christmas | The festival of Christmas is held on December 25 in the Roman Catholic Church and January 7 in the Orthodox Church. On Christmas Day, Christians celebrate the birth of Jesus, often known as the Nativity. |
| February/March | Lent | The season of Lent is the 40-day period leading up to the Easter celebration. During Lent, Christians remember Jesus's temptation in the wilderness and the events leading up to the Crucifixion. |
| March or April | Easter | Easter lasts for three days, from Friday to Sunday. On Good Friday, Christians remember Christ's Crucifixion. On Easter Sunday, they celebrate his Resurrection. |

## Ceremonies

Two of the most important ceremonies in the Christian religion are baptism and Holy Communion.

**Baptism** Baptism is also called christening. It is a ceremony to welcome a new member into the Christian faith. Some denominations baptize babies or children, while others baptize only adult Christians. In the baptism ceremony, new members come into contact with water—sometimes it is just poured over their heads, and sometimes they are completely immersed in it. This immersion in water is a symbol of the person dying and being born again into the Christian faith.

**Holy Communion** Holy Communion is also called the Eucharist or the Mass. It is a ceremony based on the Last Supper, which was held not long before the Crucifixion. At this supper, Jesus told his followers that the bread they were about to eat was his body and the wine they would drink was his blood. At Holy Communion, Christians eat bread and drink wine as a way of remembering Christ's death. The bread and blood are a symbol of the eternal life offered to Christians through Christ's death.

## Saints' days

Each day of the Christian year is dedicated to the memory of a saint—a holy person who devoted his or her life to the Christian faith. Some of the best-known saints are:

St. Valentine (February 14)—St. Valentine has become associated with love and romance.

St. David (March 1)—St. David is the patron saint of Wales.

St. Patrick (March 17)—St. Patrick is the patron saint of Ireland.

St. George (April 23)—St. George is the patron saint of England.

St. Andrew (November 30)—St. Andrew is the patron saint of Scotland.

## Approximate number of Christians worldwide

| | |
|---|---|
| 1900 | 558,000,000 |
| 1985 | 1,000,000,000 |
| 1995 | 1,928,000,000 |
| 2005 | 2,100,000,000 |

## Approximate number of Christians by continent (1995)

| | |
|---|---|
| Africa | 348,176,000 |
| Asia | 306,762,000 |
| Europe | 551,892,000 |
| South America | 448,006,000 |
| North America | 249,277,000 |
| Oceania | 23,840,000 |

# GLOSSARY

**abbot** The leader of a group of monks.

**amphitheater** A large, circular stadium used for public entertainments.

**Anglicans** People who belong to the Church of England, a branch of the Christian Protestant movement. Anglicans are mainly found in England, but there are branches of this church all over the world.

**Annunciation** The Angel Gabriel's visit to the Virgin Mary, bringing the news that she would give birth to the Son of God.

**apartheid** The political system in South Africa in which black people were separated from whites and treated as second-class citizens.

**apostles** The followers of Christ who spread his message.

**Baptists** People who belong to the Baptist Church, a branch of the Christian Protestant movement. Baptists practice adult baptism.

**barbarian** The name the Romans gave to the tribes who lived outside the Roman Empire.

**basilica** A large church.

**bishop** A senior priest in the Christian church. Bishops are in charge of all the priests and churches in a large area known as a diocese.

**Calvinists** People who belong to the Calvinist Church, a branch of the Christian Protestant movement. Calvinists believe in hell and damnation.

**catacombs** A series of tunnels under the city of Rome, where early Christians met to worship.

**congregation** A group of people gathered for worship.

**Congregationalists** Members of the Congregationalist Church, a branch of the Christian Protestant movement. Congregationalists allow each congregation to manage its own church.

**convent** A group of buildings where nuns live and work.

**creed** A statement of what someone believes.

**crucifixion** The act of putting someone to death by fastening the person to a cross and leaving him or her there to die. In the Christian religion, the Crucifixion refers to Christ's death on the cross.

**deacon** A senior priest in the early Christian church, who was in charge of practical matters, such as helping the poor.

**denominations** Branches or groups within the Christian church.

**disciples** The 12 men chosen by Christ to be his followers.

**ecumenical** Christian denominations working for unity and cooperation.

**evangelism** Taking the Christian message out into the wider world.

**excommunicated** To be expelled from the Roman Catholic Church.

**friar** A member of a Christian religious order who travels, preaching and caring for the poor and sick.

**heretic** Someone who holds beliefs that contradict the church's teachings.

**hermit** Someone who chooses to live alone and concentrate on God.

**indulgences** Pardons for sins, which were sold for money.

**liberation theology** The belief that Christians have a duty to help the poor and the suffering.

**Lutherans** People who belong to the Lutheran Church, a branch of the Christian Protestant movement. Lutheran services are very simple and are based on readings from the Bible.

**martyr** Someone who is killed or is made to suffer because of his or her beliefs.

**medieval** From the period of history known as the Middle Ages, between approximately 1000 and 1450.

**meditation** In Christianity, the practice of thinking deeply about something.

**Methodists** People who belong to the Methodist Church, a branch of the Christian Protestant movement. Methodists hold simple services with rousing hymns and passionate sermons.

**missionary** Someone who travels to a foreign land to spread his or her beliefs.

**monastery** A group of buildings where monks live and work.

**New Testament** The second part of the Bible, which tells the life of Jesus and describes how his followers spread the Christian faith.

**Nonconformists** People who belong to any of the Protestant churches, which are independent of the Roman Catholic Church.

**ordain** To permit someone to become a priest in a special ceremony.

**pagans** An archaic Christian term used to describe non-Christians who worship multiple gods.

**Pentecostal Church** A branch of the Christian Protestant movement. Pentecostal Christians hold lively services, and some of their members claim to have the gifts of prophecy and healing. They are also sometimes called Charismatic Christians.

**pilgrimage** A journey to worship at a holy place.

**pope** The head of the Roman Catholic Church.

**Presbyterians** People who belong to the Presbyterian Church, a branch of the Christian Protestant movement. Each congregation of the Presbyterian Church is governed by a group of elders.

**prophecy** Predicting what will happen in the future.

**Protestants** Christians who do not belong to the Roman Catholic or Orthodox Churches.

**Puritans** Members of a Protestant Christian movement that developed in sixteenth-century England. The Puritans dressed plainly and followed a simple form of worship.

**Quakers** Members of a Protestant Christian movement that developed in seventeenth-century England. Quakers gather in meeting houses rather than churches, and they stress the importance of quiet meditation.

**Resurrection** Christ's coming back to life, three days after his death.

**salvation** The act of being saved from sin, in order to be allowed into heaven.

**scriptures** Holy writings.

**secular** Not connected with religion.

**shrine** A holy building that often contains a sacred object, such as the remains of a saint.

**temptations** Offers of things desired as a test of a person's faith.

**Virgin Mary** The name Christians give to Mary, the mother of Jesus.

# INDEX